This book is a

Gift

From

....

To

....

Date

....

May God bless you through this book

Prayers to buy a home and settle down

PRAYERS TO BUY A HOME AND SETTLE DOWN

PRAYERS TO BUY A HOME AND SETTLE DOWN

Copyright © 2014

PRAYER M. MADUEKE

ISBN:

Prayer Publications

Unless otherwise indicated, all Scripture quotations are taken from the King James Version of the Bible, and used by permission. All emphasis within quotations is the author's additions.

First Edition, 2014

For further information of permission

1 Babatunde close, off Olaitan Street, Surulere, Lagos, Nigeria
+234 803 353 0599
Email: pastor@prayermadueke.com,
Website: www.prayermadueke.com

Dedication

This book is dedicated to people who are trusting God to buy a home and settle down happily. The Lord who sees your sincere dedication will answer your prayers Amen.

Prayers to buy a home and settle down

BOOK OVERVIEW

PRAYERS TO BUY A HOME AND SETTLE DOWN

- *A godly home: A place of rest*
- *Buying a Christian home*
- *Qualities of a good wife*
- *From earthly home to eternal home*

A GODLY HOME: A PLACE OF REST

Most Christians do not consider praying to buy their own homes. While other prayers are also important, you cannot ignore this aspect. When thinking of getting married, you should also think of building your own house or buying a home where you will live with your family. If you do not have enough finance now, start making provisions for it because it is very necessary to have a roof over your head.

> *"When they had made an end of dividing the land for inheritance by their coasts, the children of Israel gave an inheritance to Joshua the son of Nun among them: According to the word of the LORD they gave him the city which he asked, even Timnath–serah in mount Ephraim: and he built the city, and dwelt therein. These are the inheritances, which Eleazar the priest, and Joshua the son of Nun, and the heads of the fathers of the tribes of the children of Israel, divided for an inheritance by lot in Shiloh before the LORD, at the door of the tabernacle of the congregation. So they made an end of dividing the country"* (Joshua 19:49-51).

When we speak of a home of your own, we mean a personal property. You need a place where your children can call home. This is also the family house and a place of origin.

LEAVING YOUR PARENTS

When you get married, heaven opens a new chapter for your family and God commissions His angels to take you to your personal home. This is the confidence we have as Christians.

> *"[18] And the LORD God said, it is not good that the man should be alone; I will make him a help meet for him. [21] And the LORD God caused a deep sleep to fall upon Adam, and he slept: and he took one of his ribs, and closed up the flesh instead thereof; [22] And the rib, which the LORD God had taken from man, made he a woman, and brought her unto the man. [23] And Adam said, this is now bone of my bones, and flesh of my flesh: she shall be called Woman, because she was taken out of Man. [24] Therefore shall a man leave his father and his mother, and shall cleave unto his wife: and they shall be one flesh"* (Genesis 2:18, 21-24).

Nevertheless, you need to have a source of income before getting married. That is when you are qualified to think of your personal house instead of rented apartment. God has made provisions for that already. Recall that when God created Adam and Eve, He provided a home for them as well.

> *"And the LORD God planted a garden eastward in Eden; and there he put the man whom he had formed. And out of the ground made the LORD God to grow every tree that is pleasant to the sight, and good for food; the tree of life also in the midst of the garden, and the tree of knowledge of good and evil. And a river went out of Eden to water the garden; and from thence it was parted, and became into four heads. The name of the first is Pison: that is it, which compasseth the whole*

3

land of Havilah, where there is gold, And the gold of that land is good: there is bdellium and the onyx stone. And the name of the second river is Gihon: the same is it that compasseth the whole land of Ethiopia. And the name of the third river is Hiddekel: that is it, which goeth toward the east of Assyria. In addition, the fourth river is Euphrates. And the LORD God took the man, and put him into the Garden of Eden to dress it and to keep it" (Genesis 2:8-15).

As you progress in your career or business, save all the money you can and make plans to buy your own personal home. Always remember that God blessed you to be fruitful and multiply, replenish the earth and subdue it until you have dominion over other creatures.

"And God blessed them, and God said unto them, Be fruitful, and multiply, and replenish the earth, and subdue it: and have dominion over the fish of the sea, and over the fowl of the air, and over every living thing that moveth upon the earth" (Genesis 1:28).

"And he answered and said unto them, Have ye not read, that he which made them at the beginning made them male and female, And said, For this cause shall a man leave father and mother, and shall cleave to his wife: and they twain shall be one flesh? Wherefore they are no more twain, but one flesh. What therefore God hath joined together, let not man put asunder" (Matthew 19:4-6).

Most men do not struggle to fulfill God's destiny. They understand that God is there to provide help. Leaving your parents does not mean that you are no longer under their care. Rather, it lunches you into life of productivity and being a man that you are expected to be. A husband and wife should fight together and form a family.

LEAVING TO SETTLE DOWN

Leaving your parents, guardians or anybody that takes care of you, spiritually and physically, is one of the greatest battles you must fight in your life. The forces of evil that are responsible to keep people in their parents' houses are too many and would do everything in their power to keep you in bondage. When Abel decided to serve his God and established a holy family, his elder brother Cain killed him.

> *"³And in process of time it came to pass, that Cain brought of the fruit of the ground an offering unto the LORD. ⁵But unto Cain and to his offering he had not respected. In addition, Cain was very wroth, and his countenance fell. ⁶And the LORD said unto Cain, Why art thou wroth? In addition, why is thy countenance fallen? ⁷If thou doest well, shalt thou not be accepted? In addition, if thou does not well, sin lieth at the door. In addition, unto thee shall be his desire, and thou shalt rule over him. ⁸And Cain talked with Abel his brother: and it happened, when they were in the field, that Cain raised up against Abel his brother, and slew him. ⁹And the LORD said unto Cain, Where is Abel thy brother? And he said I know not: Am I my brother's keeper?"* (Genesis 4:3, 5-9).

Either Satan wants you to depend on people in his kingdom or he wants you to serve him before you are permitted to settle down in life. Abel's enemies, including Cain, his elder brother, vowed that Abel would not have freedom of worship or be a man of his own. The anger of Cain against Abel was demonically motivated. His talks and demands were demonic also. The death of Abel was more spiritual than physical.

"And it came to pass, as they journeyed from the east, that they found a plain in the land of Shinar; and they dwelt there. And they said one to another, Go to, let us make brick, and burn them thoroughly. In addition, they had brick for stone, and slime had they for mortar. And they said, Go to, let us build us a city and a tower, whose top may reach unto heaven; and let us make us a name, lest we be scattered abroad upon the face of the whole earth" (<u>Genesis 11:2-4</u>).

Evil forces that prevent people from leaving their parents and settling down according to God's will would only allow you to settle down if you would accept to remain under their bondage. They want your independence according to their terms. Before they allow someone to settle down, they want that person to abandon God and serve devil. They want to ensure that more people build houses and settle down without God in their lives.

If you are under the curse of devil, he cannot permit you to involve God when searching for the right person. When you want to build or buy a house, he wants you to do it without involving God. However, when you insist in marrying the right wife, get children and get a good job, you are in for his troubles. The solution is to come out of the curse of devil and come under the covenant of Jesus and His blood.

Devil does not want you to settle down the right way. He would always attack with all manner of problems. He wants to attack your marriage, job, health and finances or even manipulate you to buy a wrong house where he is in-charge. In such houses, you would experience incessant attacks from witches and diverse problems. You see yourself face to face with divorce and separation.

Devil does not want Christians to settle down the right way. Millions of people that have left their parents are not settled in peace yet. It is not good to buy a home and have no peace. A home is made up of a husband, wife, children and other members of the family. However, a home cannot be what God wants it to be if there is no love in that home.

> *"Husbands, love your wives, even as Christ also loved the church, and gave himself for it; That he might sanctify and cleanse it with the washing of water by the word, That he might present it to himself a glorious church, not having spot, or wrinkle, or any such thing; but that it should be holy and without blemish. So ought men to love their wives as their own bodies. He that loved his wife loved himself. For no man ever yet hated his own flesh; but nourished and cherished it, even as the Lord the church: For we are members of his body, of his flesh, and of his bones. For this cause shall a man leave his father and mother, and shall be joined unto his wife, and they two shall be one flesh. This is a great mystery: but I speak concerning Christ and the church. Nevertheless let every one of you in particular so love his wife even as himself; and the wife see that she reverence her husband"* (Ephesians 5:25-33).

A husband must love his wife as God commanded. He must die to self. He must be a sacrificial and holy husband, a sharing father and an understanding leader of the family. He must share his love equal to the members of his family so that there is no room for animosity, struggle and fight. Marriage should be nothing but a perfect and glorious union.

"That they may teach the young women to be sober, to love their husbands, to love their children" (Titus 2:4).

"8Owe no man anything, but to love one another: for he that loved another hath fulfilled the law. 10 Love worked no ill to his neighbor: therefore love is the fulfilling of the law" (Romans 13:8, 10).

For any family to achieve its glorious destiny, love must be at the center. You can do everything to buy a home, get good furniture and other comfortable things but if there is no love, you do not have a home. When we speak of a Christian home, we mean a home where the husband has modeled the love Christ has for the church, and shepherded for the sheep. A good husband sees no danger in losing his wife provided he does not love his wife more than he loves God.

"Now there is at Jerusalem by the sheep market a pool, which is called in the Hebrew tongue Bethesda, having five porches" (John 5:2).

"Now there is at Jerusalem by the sheep market a pool, which is called in the Hebrew tongue Bethesda, having five porches" (John 13:1).

"We know that we have passed from death unto life, because we love the brethren. He that loved not his brother abideth in death. Whosoever hated his brother is a murderer: and ye know that no murderer hath eternal life abiding in him. Hereby perceive we the love of God, because he laid down his life for us: and we ought to lay down our lives for the brethren. But whoso hath this world's good, and seeth his brother have need, and shutteth up his bowels of compassion from him, how dwelled the love of God in him? My little

children, let us not love in word, neither in tongue; but in deed nor in truth" (<u>1 John 3:14-18</u>).

God is searching for a husband that is willing to deny himself, bear toil and trial to provide and care for his wife, defend her and protect his household. When we speak of buying a home, it is more than buying your house physically. We mean securing your home spiritually before purchasing it. A physical home filled with good things without love is just a house and a place where enemies live together.

Prayers to buy a home and settle down

BUYING A CHRISTIAN HOME

From the beginning of time, God determined it was good for His people to have a good place to live. That was why He created the Garden of Eden and put Adam and his wife in it. God wanted a place where He would rest each time He wished. He planned it, purposed it and provided it from the beginning.

> *"18And the LORD God said, it is not good that the man should be alone; I will make him a help meet for him. 20And Adam gave names to all cattle and to the fowl of the air, and to every beast of the field; but for Adam there was not found a helpmeet for him. 22And the rib, which the LORD God had taken from man, made him a woman, and brought her unto the man. 24Therefore shall a man leave his father and his mother, and shall cleave unto his wife: and they shall be one flesh"* (Genesis 2:18, 20, 22, 24).

> *"For this cause shall a man leave his father and mother, and shall be joined unto his wife, and they two shall be one flesh"* (Ephesians 5:31).

God said it was not good to have a home without a wife. What He pronounced as *not good* in the days of Adam is still not good today. You can have all that you desired for in your life like cattle, birds, land, servants, etc. However, if you do not have a wife, your home is not complete.

Most young and unmarried men think that what they need most is money in order to get married but that is not true. You need God first, who then would give you a wife, the flesh of your flesh and bone of your bone, and wealth. In addition, some men would do

11

everything to get money and build a house before thinking of getting a wife. That may be good but the best thing is for a man to know God. When you know God, He provides you a home and a wife to make you complete.

When you strive to get a home without God in it, the devil may give you his daughter to marry. But when you have God without a home, He is able to give you a wife and a home. Therefore, the most important thing is that everything you have comes from the Lord. Some men have killed and done many evil things in order to get whatever they wanted. Eventually, they got it but do not have peace.

Buying a home or building a house without God is regrettable and useless. Wife, home, money or material things without God in them would constitute a big problem. Only God can give you a good home. The sons of Noah had all they needed to own physical homes, yet they failed.

> *"And the LORD came down to see the city and the tower, which the children of men builder. And the LORD said, Behold, the people is one, and they have all one language; and this they begin to do: and now nothing will be restrained from them, which they have imagined to do. Go to, let us go down, and there confound their language, that they may not understand one another's speech. So the LORD scattered them abroad from thence upon the face of all the earth: and they left off to build the city"* (<u>Genesis 11:5-8</u>).

Anything you are doing without God in it will fail eventually. Many people have closed their ears and eyes to the gospel. They struggle to get money, job and build houses here and there without God. That was what the sons of Noah did but they failed. You may have defrauded people, killed and did all manner of evil things to get whatever you wanted but you will not have peace. Others, after doing all manner of evil things, would invite God to bless their evil wealth. They look for the most beautiful, educated and intelligent women to marry. Things may be working for you now but someday, problem would set in because you have refused to involve God from the beginning.

> *"Send thine hand from above; rid me, and deliver me out of great waters, from the hand of strange children"* (Psalms 144:7).

As a woman, you may be searching for a man with wealth. You may find such man eventually. However, if he does not know God, you may live a miserable life on earth. Some men are often kind to other women but wicked to their wives. In such homes, no matter what you have in it, it cannot be a home. Some peoples' homes are like wrestling field, drinking spot or graveyard. A husband that does not have time for his wife has no home. A husband that does not love his wife has no home. A husband that does not protect his wife has no home. A husband that beats his wife has no home. He may have the best business, best house in the city and the largest bank account but he has no home.

A husband that cannot provide for his family and control his children has no home. A husband that cannot guide, protect, provide and teach his children has no home. He may be seen as the head but he is only a figurehead. Such husband, even when he is fully involved in the church but is not in-charge of affairs in his house, he has no home. A head that does not stay with the body is no longer the head. A committed head

13

of the family stays with the body until death. That is how a good husband should be to his wife and the members of the family.

> *"For the husband is the head of the wife, even as Christ is the head of the church: and he is the savior of the body"* (Ephesians 5:23).

> *"But I would have you know, that the head of every man is Christ; and the head of the woman is the man; and the head of Christ is God"* (1 Corinthians 11:3).

> *"One that ruleth well his own house, having his children in subjection with all gravity; (For if a man know not how to rule his own house, how shall he take care of the church of God?)"* (1 Timothy 3:4-5).

Naturally, a man feeds, protects, cleanses and cares for his body. He takes care of any part of his organ that is sick and allows his legs and hands to rest when they are tired. He cares for his body, grants them rest, and sympathizes with his body when it is weak. He allows his eyes to close for sleep when he is tired. It is stupidity for someone to use his hands to beat himself, or someone to pluck out his eyes. Such hand is not normal and such a person is not normal.

A man that beats his wife or exposes her weaknesses to his parents and outsiders is not a good head. No normal husband can abuse his wife and remain normal. Many beautiful houses are not homes because the inhabitants are not with God who is the head of the universe and the creator of heaven and earth.

QUALITIES OF A GOOD WIFE

A good wife accepts the divinely ordained headship of her husband not because the husband is good and merits it but because God ordained it. She submits to her husband as unto the Lord in all things.

> "Wives, submit yourselves unto your own husbands, as unto the Lord. For the husband is the head of the wife, even as Christ is the head of the church: and he is the savior of the body. Therefore as the church is subject unto Christ, so let the wives be to their own husbands in everything" (Ephesians 5:22-24).

> "Likewise, ye wives, be in subjection to your own husbands; that, if any obey not the word, they also may without the word be won by the conversation of the wives; While they behold your chaste conversation coupled with fear" (1 Peter 3:1-2).

> "Wives, submit yourselves unto your own husbands, as it is fit in the Lord" (Colossians 3:18).

A Christian wife is supposed to be tender, lovely, gentle and meek at home and everywhere. It is her duty to obey and submit herself to her husband except in what is contrary to faith and pure conscience.

> "But Peter and John answered and said unto them, Whether it be right in the sight of God to hearken unto you more than unto God, judge ye" (Acts 4:19).

> *"Then Peter and the other apostles answered and said we ought to obey God rather than men"* (<u>Acts 5: 29</u>).

She submits in domestic matters, family rules and in everything that is godly. The husband has the right to direct things while the wife submits. In submitting, it has to be as unto the Lord and not in a grudge as if she is doing favor to her husband.

> *"But let it be the hidden man of the heart, in that which is not corruptible, even the ornament of a meek and quiet spirit, which is in the sight of God of great price. For after this manner in the old time the holy women also, who trusted in God, adorned themselves, being in subjection unto their own husbands: Even as Sara obeyed Abraham, calling him lord: whose daughters ye are, as long as ye do well, and are not afraid with any amazement"* (<u>1 Peter 3:4-6</u>).

A good wife lives with meek and quiet spirit in the sight of God and all men. Esther learnt how to be obedient and submissive from her uncle, Mordecai, after she lost her father. She obeyed her uncle and submitted to all his charges. When the king saw her quality and meek spirit, he preferred Esther above other virgins. She obtained grace and favor in the sight of the king, and was crowned the Queen. With obedience, meek and humble spirit, Esther found favor before the king who granted all her request.

> *"And it fell on a day, that Elisha passed to Shunem, where was a great woman; and she constrained him to eat bread. Therefore, it was that as soft as he passed by, he turned in thither to eat bread. And she said unto her husband, Behold now, I perceive that this is an holy man of*

16

God, which passed by us continually. Let us make a little chamber, I pray thee, on the wall; and let us set for him there a bed, and a table, and a stool, and a candlestick: and it shall be, when he cometh to us that he shall turn in thither" (2 Kings 4:8-10).

Likewise, the woman of Shunem is worthy of emulation. She could have been providing for her family and built their house. Yet, she did not contend for her husband's position. She was the one who saw the need to accommodate Elisha in their home, but she sought for her husband's approval first. She demonstrated a life of a submissive woman.

Another submissive woman worthy of emulation is Elizabeth. Her character radiated the character of God. She was a righteous woman who walked in the commandments of God without blame. Though she had no child, there was peace and divine presence in her home even at her old age.

"[5]There was in the days of Herod, the king of Judea, a certain priest named Zacharias, of the course of Abia: and his wife was of the daughters of Aaron, and her name was Elisabeth. [6]And they were both righteous before God, walking in all the commandments and ordinances of the Lord blameless. [7]And they had no child, because that Elisabeth was barren, and they both were now well stricken in years. [23]And it came to pass, that, as soon as the days of his ministration were accomplished, he departed to his own house. [24]And after those days his wife Elisabeth conceived, and hid herself five months, saying, [25]Thus hath the Lord dealt with me in the days wherein he looked on me, to take away my reproach among men. [57]Now Elisabeth's full time

came that she should be delivered; and she brought forth a son. [58]And her neighbors and her cousins heard how the Lord had showed great mercy upon her; and they rejoiced with her. [59]And it came to pass, that on the eighth day they came to circumcise the child; and they called him Zacharias, after the name of his father. [60]And his mother answered and said, Not so; but he shall be called John. [61]And they said unto her, there is none of thy kindred that is called by this name. [62]And they made signs to his father, how he would have him called. [63]And he asked for a writing table, and wrote, saying, His name is John. In addition, they marveled all. [64]And his mouth was opened immediately, and his tongue loosed, and he spake, and praised God" (<u>Luke 1:5-7</u>; <u>23-25</u>, <u>57-64</u>).

At old age, Elizabeth was still humble, meek and submissive to her husband and God. God visited her at her old age and she conceived. Her joy was complete at the birth of their son, John. There are other women of noble character in the Bible like Mary the mother of Christ (*See* <u>Luke 2:19</u>; <u>Matthew 2:13-14</u>, <u>19-22</u>; <u>Luke 2:41-48</u>).

Some of the qualities of a good wife include reverence for God and her husband, humility, meekness, quietness, loving, diligence, dependable, prayerful and hospitality. When you have a loving and submissive wife, and obedient children, your home would be heaven on earth.

As a wife, you may not have all these qualities but believe that things will change for the best as you pray through selected prayer points at the end of this book. With the grace of God, you can bring these qualities into your home today. If you do not have the finance you need, begin to pray and God would provide finances for you to buy a home. If you have finances already, may God give you the wisdom to buy a home in a place where you will never lack God's presence forever.

FROM EARTHLY HOME TO ETERNAL HOME

The earthly home is a shadow or model of our heavenly home. Therefore, if your earthly home lacks the presence of God, how can you partake in the heavenly home? Ask God to come into your home today as we wait for the return of our Lord Jesus Christ.

> *"Let not your heart be troubled: ye believe in God, believe also in me. In my Father's house are many mansions: if it were not so, I would have told you. I go to prepare a place for you. And if I go and prepare a place for you, I will come again, and receive you unto myself; that where I am, there ye may be also. And whither I go ye know, and the way ye know"* (John 14:1-4).

Saints who maintained their faith on earth would be home with Christ eternally. In heaven, believers will enjoy fellowship, rest, holiness, service and glory with God forever. Even true believers who did not acquire a physical home on earth will reign with other believers of all ages as citizens of the new heaven. No matter how comfortable, peaceable, restful or enjoyable your home here on earth is, you have a better home in heaven. We are only ambassadors on earth.

> *"For our conversation is in heaven; from whence also we look for the Savior, the Lord Jesus Christ: Who shall change our vile body, that it may be fashioned like unto his glorious body, according to the working whereby he is able even to subdue all things unto himself"* (Philippians 3:20-21).

> *"Now then we are ambassadors for Christ, as though God did beseech you by us: we pray you*

in Christ's stead, be ye reconciled to God" (2 Corinthians 5:20).

It is good to own a home here on earth. It is your right because the earth and its fullness belong to our Father in heaven. However, your focus should be the heavenly home. We are just strangers here on earth. Our home is in heaven. Our Father is in heaven. Our Savior is there. Our homes, names, lives, treasures, affections, hearts, inheritance and citizenship are all there. Jesus is the only way to paradise, our heavenly home.

> *"Thomas saith unto him, Lord, we know not whither thou goest; and how can we know the way? Jesus saith unto him, I am the way, the truth, and the life: no man cometh unto the Father, but by me"* (John 14:5-6).

If you are not born-again yet, then you are not at peace with God through Jesus Christ. Therefore, you will not come to heaven. Those that will live in the heavenly home are those born of the Spirit here on earth and lead a good spiritual homes where Christ reigns.

> *"And I heard a great voice out of heaven saying, Behold, the tabernacle of God is with men, and he will dwell with them, and they shall be his people, and God himself shall be with them, and be their God. And God shall wipe away all tears from their eyes; and there shall be no more death, neither sorrow, nor crying, neither shall there be any more pain: for the former things are passed away"* (Revelation 21:3-4).

> *"And there shall be no more curse: but the throne of God and of the Lamb shall be in it; and his servants shall serve him: And they shall see his*

face; and his name shall be in their foreheads" (Revelation 22:3-4).

Your name must be written in the book of life here on earth with a testimony of a spiritual home on earth before you can be admitted into the heavenly home. The fearful, unbelieving, abominable, murderers, whoremongers, fornicators, adulterers, sorcerers, witches and wizards, occultists and all those that use familiar spirits, idolaters and all liars will not be allowed to enter into the home in heaven.

> *"⁸But the fearful, and unbelieving, and the abominable, and murderers, and whoremongers, and sorcerers, and idolaters, and all liars, shall have their part in the lake which burnet with fire and brimstone: which is the second death. ²⁷And there shall in no wise enter into it anything that defiled, neither whatsoever worked abomination, or maketh a lie: but they which are written in the Lamb's book of life"* (Revelation 21:8, 27).

> *"And whosoever was not found written in the book of life was cast into the lake of fire"* (Revelation 20:15).

> *"For without are dogs, and sorcerers, and whoremongers, and murderers, and idolaters, and whosoever loved and maketh a lie"* (Revelation 22:15).

Other references: (John 9:18-22; Matthew 10:33-36; John 3:18-20, 36; Leviticus 18:21-27; Deuteronomy 22:5; Proverbs 6:16-19; 1 John 3:15; Matthew 5:27-30; Deuteronomy 18:9-14; 1 Samuel 28:5-11; 1 Chronicles 10:13-14; Isaiah 8:19; Exodus 20:3-5; 1 John 5:21).

It is not possible, no matter how clever you are, to enter into heaven and desecrate the eternal home of the

Lord's children. No sinner would be allowed in to stain or desecrate the holy home of the bride and the lamb. All sinners shall be banished from the presence of God and from the eternal home of the saints forever. They shall be cast into the lake of fire forever. In the new heaven, we shall hunger or thirst no more.

> *"There is a river, the streams whereof shall make glad the city of God, the holy place of the tabernacles of the most High"* (Psalms 46:4).

> *"And he showed me a pure river of water of life, clear as crystal, proceeding out of the throne of God and of the Lamb. In the midst of the street of it, and on either side of the river, was there the tree of life, which bare twelve manner of fruits, and yielded her fruit every month: and the leaves of the tree were for the healing of the nations. And there shall be no more curse: but the throne of God and of the Lamb shall be in it; and his servants shall serve him: And they shall see his face; and his name shall be in their foreheads. And there shall be no night there; and they need no candle, neither light of the sun; for the Lord God gives them light: and they shall reign forever and ever"* (Revelation 22:1-5).

We shall fast or cry no more. We shall have access to the water of life in our eternal home as a continuous reminder that Christ truly gives the water of life. In our eternal home, the tree of life yields a different type of fruit. It would be a great disappointment for you to know this and yet not experience it. Are you going to allow the devil or the little enjoyment on earth to deny you of your eternal rest in the eternal home? It would be a great and eternal loss. It will not be your portion in Jesus name.

"Jesus saith unto them, Bring of the fish which ye have now caught. Simon Peter went up, and drew the net to land full of great fishes, an hundred and fifty and three: and for all there were so many, yet was not the net broken. Jesus saith unto them, Come and dine. In addition, none of the disciples durst ask him, who art thou? Knowing that it was the Lord. Jesus then cometh, and taketh bread, and giveth them, and fish likewise. This is now the third time that Jesus showed himself to his disciples, after that he was risen from the dead" (John 21:10-14).

"[15]And he said unto them, With desire I have desired to eat this Passover with you before I suffer: [16]For I say unto you, I will not any more eat thereof, until it be fulfilled in the kingdom of God. [17]And he took the cup, and gave thanks, and said, Take this, and divide it among yourselves: [18]For I say unto you, I will not drink of the fruit of the vine, until the kingdom of God shall come. [29]And I appoint unto you a kingdom, as my Father hath appointed unto me; [30]That ye may eat and drink at my table in my kingdom, and sit on thrones judging the twelve tribes of Israel" (Luke 22:15-18, 29-30).

The leaves of the tree of life will heal all that would come into the heavenly home. There shall be no curse, no more death or pains.

"In the midst of the street of it, and on either side of the river, was there the tree of life, which bare twelve manner of fruits, and yielded her fruit every month: and the leaves of the tree were for the healing of the nations. And there shall be no more curses: but the throne of God and of the

Lamb shall be in it; and his servants shall serve him" (Revelation 22:2-3).

"And God shall wipe away all tears from their eyes; and there shall be no more death, neither sorrow, nor crying, neither shall there be any more pain: for the former things are passed away" (Revelation 21:4).

The tree of life will ensure joy and health to all that would enter into the eternal home. Our Lord Jesus is the designer of this city and He promised to build it with His Father and afterwards returns to take us home. The city is full of blazing and brilliance glory of God. Everything in that city is clear as crystal with good design and perfect symmetry. It will be able to contain billions of people with billions of empty spaces left. You cannot afford to miss this eternal home.

"In my Father's house are many mansions: if it were not so, I would have told you. I go to prepare a place for you" (John 14:2).

"Because strait is the gate, and narrow is the way, which leaded unto life, and few there be that find it" (Matthew 7:14).

Unfortunately, many will not be there. Where will you be and where will you spend your eternity?

"[11]He that is unjust, let him be unjust still: and he which is filthy, let him be filthy still: and he that is righteous, let him be righteous still: and he that is holy, let him be holy still. [15]For without are dogs, and sorcerers, and whoremongers, and murderers, and idolaters, and whosoever loved and maketh a lie. [18] For I testify unto every man that hearten the words of the prophecy of this book, If any man shall add unto these things, God

25

shall add unto him the plagues that are written in this book: [19] *And if any man shall take away from the words of the book of this prophecy, God shall take away his part out of the book of life, and out of the holy city, and from the things which are written in this book"* (Revelation 22:11, 15, 18-19).

"The wicked shall be turned into hell, and all the nations that forget God" (Psalms 9:17).

Unrepentant sinners will separate from God forever. They will be thrown into the lake of fire forever. However, the redeemed, those who are made righteous through the blood of Jesus Christ will remain righteous forever while all unrepentant sinners will retain their evil and sinful nature forever.

"And he stewed me a pure river of water of life, clear as crystal, proceeding out of the throne of God and of the Lamb" (Revelation 22:1).

"Come unto me, all ye that labor and are heavy laden and I will give you rest. Take my yoke upon you, and learn of me; for I am meek and lowly in heart: and ye shall find rest unto your souls. For my yoke is easy, and my burden is light" (Matthew 11:28-30).

This may be your last chance and final invitation to accept Jesus into your life. Therefore, I beg you to respond now. Give your life to Christ, repent, confess all your sins and forsake them. Life is too short. Your end on earth is much closer than you think. You need to live a spiritual life on earth in a godly home. Start building your home today.

Prayers to buy a home and settle down

"But seek ye first the kingdom of God, and his righteousness; and all these things shall be added unto you" (<u>Matthew 6:33</u>).

PRAYERS TO BUY A HOME AND SETTLE DOWN

Bible reference: Joshua 21:43-45

Begin with praise and worship

1. Father Lord, help me to locate a home, get money and buy it to Your glory, in the name of Jesus.

2. Any strongman that lives in my land of promise, die, in the name of Jesus.

3. Lord Jesus, provide money for me to buy a home this year, in the name of Jesus.

4. I receive the ability to start saving money to purchase a house, in the name of Jesus.

5. Any power that is militating against my savings for buying a house, die, in the name of Jesus.

6. I command every demon that is attacking my savings to die, in the name of Jesus.

7. O Lord, give me wisdom and divine ability to save enough money to buy a good house, in the name of Jesus.

8. I destroy problems that were designed to swallow my finances for the new house, in the name of Jesus.

9. O Lord, arise and increase my income this year, in the name of Jesus.

10. I refuse to enter into any trouble that would stop me from buying a house, in the name of Jesus.

11. Let any evil tongue that is rising against my plans to buy a house receive fire, in the name of Jesus.

12. Father Lord, give me financial explosion this year by fire, in the name of Jesus.

13. Let the handwriting of my enemies be erased that I may buy my house, in the name of Jesus.

14. Let any spiritual house in my land of promise, collapse in the name of Jesus.

15. Let spiritual owners of my new house release it and die, in the name of Jesus.

16. Every evil sacrifice that was done in my house for my sake, expire, in the name of Jesus.

17. Any evil personality that is living inside my new house, die, in the name of Jesus.

18. I paralyze evil powers that have vowed to keep me as a tenant forever, in the name of Jesus.

19. O Lord, empower me financially to buy a new house of Your choice without debts, in the name of Jesus.

20. I break and loose myself from the power of financial and material poverty, in the name of Jesus.

21. I trample upon every problem that is preventing me from buying a family house this year, in the name of Jesus.

22. I lift every satanic embargo that was placed upon my new house, in the name of Jesus.

23. Any evil activity that is preventing me from buying a new house this year is frustrated, in the name of Jesus.

24. O Lord, arise and finance my new house at the right time, in the name of Jesus.

25. O Lord, help me to buy a house in a right place where Your peace reigns, in the name of Jesus.

26. I chase away evil spirits that are residing at the location of my new house, in the name of Jesus.

27. O Lord, lead me to a place where I would live and call my own, in the name of Jesus.

28. Let every opposition that is standing against my new house disappear, in the name of Jesus.

29. O Lord, empower me to buy a house at a place and city of choice, in the name of Jesus.

30. Let the angels of God walk me into the right place to buy a house, in the name of Jesus.

31. Let spiritual residents of my divinely new house vacate by fire, in the name of Jesus.

32. Every satanic soldier that is militating against my plans to buy a house at the right place, die, in the name of Jesus.

33. Father Lord, sponsor me financially to purchase a house at the right place, in the name of Jesus.

34. Any power that is forcing me to buy a house at a wrong place, die, in the name of Jesus.

35. Let my God arise and create an opportunity for me to buy the right house, in the name of Jesus.

36. Any power that has vowed to confine me to my parent's house, die, in the name of Jesus.

37. I receive power to leave my parents and buy a personal house, in the name of Jesus.

38. Any attack that is going on against my business or work, be frustrated, in the name of Jesus.

39. Let household witchcraft powers that have vowed that I will not own a house be disgraced, in the name of Jesus.

40. Any evil altar that has arrested my house spiritually, release it now, in the name of Jesus.

41. I disgrace evil personalities that have vowed that I will never own a house, in the name of Jesus.

42. I discard satanic pressures to buy a house at a wrong place, in the name of Jesus.

43. I break every yoke or bondage upon my life not to buy a personal house, in the name of Jesus.

44. I refuse to do evil in order to prosper before I buy a house, in the name of Jesus.

45. I receive power not to do evil before I buy a house, in the name of Jesus.

46. I refuse to buy a house without involving God fully, in the name of Jesus.

47. I refuse to pack into a house where evil spirits are living, in the name of Jesus.

48. Every enemy of God in the new house I want to buy, vacate by force, in the name of Jesus.

49. Let the hosts of heaven provide and lead me to buy a Christian home, in the name of Jesus.

50. I refuse to get a house on earth that will cause me to miss heaven, in the name of Jesus.

51. Father Lord, help me to buy a house where only You will reign, in the name of Jesus.

52. Father Lord, empower my wife/husband to beautify our new home, in the name of Jesus.

53. Let my home be the habitation of God and His saints on earth, in the name of Jesus.

54. Let my wife, husband and children attract divine presence at home, in the name of Jesus.

55. Let everything that would perfect my home according to God's Word appear by force, in the name of Jesus.

56. Let every enemy of my home be expose and disgraced, in the name of Jesus.

57. I hand over the keys of my new home to God, in the name of Jesus.

58. Any invitation that was given to devil and his agents, I withdraw you, in the name of Jesus.

59. I disgrace any stubborn demon that has vowed not to leave my home to death, in the name of Jesus.

60. Let the beauty of the Lord possess my new home, in the name of Jesus.

61. Any good thing my home is lacking even before I buy it, appear, in the name of Jesus.

62. I bring God, the host of heaven and every good thing into my home before I buy it, in the name of Jesus.

63. Let evil messengers that were assigned to my new home be frustrated, in the name of Jesus.

64. Any satanic giant in my home, die before I buy the house, in the name of Jesus.

65. Let warriors from heaven march into my home before I come in to settle, in the name of Jesus.

66. Let any Cain in my new home die, in the name of Jesus.

67. I destroy every bad thing in my new home, in the name of Jesus.

68. Let any evil in my home face divine defeats, in the name of Jesus.

69. Let the angels of God invade my home before I buy it, in the name of Jesus.

70. Let any Amorite, Canaanite and other Hittites in my home be destroyed, in the name of Jesus.

71. Thou death from God, kill every enemy of my family before I move in with my family, in the name of Jesus.

72. Father Lord, take me into my home without defilement or pollution, in the name of Jesus.

73. Owners of evil load in my home, appear and carry your loads, in the name of Jesus.

74. Let soldiers from heaven conduct a search in my home and chase evil away before my arrival, in the name of Jesus.

75. I refuse to enter into covenant with devil and his agents in my new home, in the name of Jesus.

Thank You So Much!

Beloved, I hope you enjoyed this book as much as I believe God has touched your heart today. I cannot thank you enough for your continued support for this prayer ministry.

I appreciate you so much for taking out time to read this wonderful prayer book, and if you have an extra second, I would love to hear what you think about this book.

Please, do share your testimonies with me by sending emails to pastor@prayermadueke.com, or through the social media at www.facebook.com/prayer.madueke. I invite you also to www.prayermadueke.com to view other books I have written on various issues of life, especially on marriage, family, sexual problems and money.

I will be delighted to partner with you in organized crusades, ceremonies, marriages and Marriage seminars, special events, church ministration and fellowship for the advancement of God's Kingdom here on earth.

Thank you again, and I wish you success in your life.

God bless you.

In Christ,

Prayer M. Madueke

OTHER BOOKS BY PRAYER M. MADUEKE

- *21/40 Nights Of Decrees And Your Enemies Will Surrender*
- *Confront And Conquer*
- *Tears in Prison*
- *35 Special Dangerous Decrees*
- *The Reality of Spirit Marriage*
- *Queen of Heaven*
- *Leviathan the Beast*
- *100 Days Prayer To Wake Up Your Lazarus*
- *Dangerous Decrees To Destroy Your Destroyers*
- *The spirit of Christmas*
- *More Kingdoms To Conquer*
- *Your Dream Directory*
- *The Sword Of New Testament Deliverance*
- *Alphabetic Battle For Unmerited Favors*
- *Alphabetic Character Deliverance*
- *Holiness*
- *The Witchcraft Of The Woman That Sits Upon Many Waters*
- *The Operations Of The Woman That Sits Upon Many Waters*
- *Powers To Pray Once And Receive Answers*
- *Prayer Riots To Overthrow Divorce*
- *Prayers To Get Married Happily*
- *Prayers To Keep Your Marriage Out of Troubles*
- *Prayers For Conception And Power To Retain*
- *Prayer Retreat – Prayers to Possess Your Year*
- *Prayers for Nation Building*
- *Organized student in a disorganized school*
- *Welcome to Campus*
- *Alone with God (10 series)*

CONTACTS

AFRICA
#1 Babatunde close,
Off Olaitan Street, Surulere
Lagos, Nigeria
+234 803 353 0599
pastor@prayermadueke.com

#Plot 1791, No. 3 Ijero Close,
Flat 2, Area 1,
Garki 1 - FCT, Abuja
+234 807 065 4159

IRELAND
Ps Emmanuel Oko
#84 Thornfield Square
Cloudalkin D22
Ireland
Tel: +353 872 820 909, +353 872 977 422
aghaoko2003@yahoo.com

EUROPE/SCHENGEN
Collins Kwame
#46 Felton Road
Barking
Essex IG11 7XZ GB
Tel: +44 208 507 8083, +44 787 703 2386, +44 780 703 6916
aghaoko2003@yahoo.com

Printed in Great Britain
by Amazon

62196053R00028